AF386690

Prospectus

Prospectus

1988–2010

Forty-two works

By Ben Kinmont

CONTENTS

Preface

I wrote the first *Prospectus* at the suggestion of Christophe Cherix, a friend with whom I shared an interest in the history of conceptual art and the role of documentation and archives. At the time Christophe was working at the Cabinet des estampes in Geneva and he and Lionel Bovier had just started a publishing company called JRP Editions. To help bolster support for the book Christophe suggested bringing the Centre national de l'édition et de l'art imprimé (CNEAI) into the project and so he introduced me to Sylvie Boulanger, with whom I would work again later in 2002 (see below). The first edition of *Prospectus* covered projects from 1988 to 2000 and is now out of print. I am grateful to Christophe, Lionel, and Sylvie for the interest and encouragement they showed me ten years ago.

When Christophe brought up the idea of a book, I had in fact written most of the project descriptions already. In the middle of the 1990s, when I was finished with a project on the street or in someone's home, I would write a description of the experience to let my friends know what I had been up to. So when Christophe suggested a book it seemed logical to gather together these descriptions as well as write up those which were missing, the goal being to make them available to others beyond my circle of friends.

I chose the title *Prospectus* to refer to a proposal or a suggestion for things to come. My projects have always followed a question-based practice, one where I am trying to explore the possibilities and limitations of an activity and what can and cannot happen from the different value structures that occupy our lives. In the context of this investigation the title *Prospectus* reveals my optimism that there are still places in which to do things and that there are still things to be done.

This *Prospectus* differs from the first in that it has been expanded to include new projects since 2000 as well as a few others that I had unintentionally omitted. The first edition was printed offset in Switzerland with a signature of photographic reproductions. In the current edition, the text is printed letterpress with individual pieces of lead type and the signature of illustrations, while also printed letterpress, uses polymer plates, a more recent printing technology more akin to woodblock printing than offset. These new illustrations are facsimiles of documents taken directly from the project archives and effectively become an extension of the archives themselves. The current edition is also accompanied by a much smaller, artist's edition, one where each book is numbered and signed and comes with one of the forms of lead type from which the book was printed. The size of this edition is equal to the number of projects in the book, forty-two.

Ben Kinmont
Sebastopol, November 2010

PROJECT DESCRIPTIONS

Project can be repeated means that the project can be made again with or without letting me know and with or without my involvement.

Carl Andre killed his wife.

They were both abusive to themselves, and he had spent so much time talking about accessible work. And then there was the issue of family, as artists and if it was possible.

Olivier Mosset first bought this piece; but then, when Carl Andre gave money to Julian Pretto to help him during the last months of his life, Olivier wanted to trade the piece. He had also become friends with Carl in the meantime. I, too, was interested in how the piece meant to me now, having heard about Carl's support of Julian. So the piece grew into new questions.

1988 plastic letters on a wall (the same year that Andre was acquitted). 1995 notes added concerning piece's return and trade. Project cannot be repeated. In the collection of the artist.

Kitchen table.

I was washing dishes and needing to make dinner. Also, trying to get social sculpture, a beginning point for this project, to include the mundane, the accessible moments of maintenance and finding them that afternoon.

1989. In my home. Unedited video, 23 minutes long. Project can be repeated. Olivier Mosset Collection.

I am for you, Ich bin für Sie.

William James had talked about the shiftiness of truth, about its lack of a single center. So, to test my idea about the third sculpture, I wrote catalytic texts and gave them out on the street. Most didn't view it as art and the project evolved through their understanding and criticism. Most importantly, you could have walked by and not even noticed that it was going on.

Archive begun 1990. New York City: Prince and Broadway, Court and Joralemon, Thompson between Spring and Prince, 5th Avenue and 57th Street. Cologne: Rudolfplatz, Wallraffplatz, Ehrenstrasse and Apostelenstrasse, Olivandenhof and Zeppelinstrasse. 22 hours and 45 minutes spent on the street. 11,750 catalytic texts given. Project can be repeated. Archive in the collection of the artist.

I trust you, I take you.

There were too many people and it was my first time in front of others making work. At the time, what I called the Carl Andre dilemma, of words and practice, seemed our condition; so, I inscribed two circles on the wall, using our largest salad bowl. Around one I wrote "I trust you" and around the other "I take you." Then, at a table, I sat and drew the same onto envelopes, using a ballpoint pen and a drinking glass. Finally someone asked if he could have one, so I gave it to him, asking that he leave his signature in exchange for the sculpture.

1991. Four Walls, Brooklyn. Forty-nine people took envelopes and left their signatures. Project can be repeated. Location of framed envelopes and signatures unknown; photographic documentation in the collection of the artist.

Waffles for an opening.

Many years later, I read that Robert Filliou had thought that art about life was not so important for what it did for art, but for what it did for life.

For a two-month period people came to our house for waffle breakfasts. I was thinking about if it was safe for my family, how many would come, and who was trusting most. My biggest surprise was how my friends didn't come, but strangers did. We signed the paper plates as a thanks for coming and I started to see it as the gift sculpture object.

Archive begun 1990. New York City. White Columns and my home over thirty-one days. 432 people took invitations. Thirty-two people ate waffles. Project can be repeated. Archive in the Bill Arning Collection.

A Prayer for greater compassion in the art world.

I spoke with various priests about whether prayer could be sculpture. Then, in 1994, over lunch, one told me that he had just reached the conclusion that prayer was about paying attention. Afterwards I wrote a prayer on my studio wall and then chipped it off.

Archive begun 1991. New York City. Project can be repeated. Archive in the collection of the artist.

I need you.

While on the street, their time was to describe the space in between; their trust was to give me their signature and a means of contacting them. I fulfilled my promise by giving them the proceeds of the archive's sale. One participant put the check in a frame whereas another, who was living in a shelter at the time but had since moved on, never received his share of the proceeds.

Archive begun 1992. 96th and Broadway, 16th and Eighth Avenue, and Murray and Broadway, New York City. Four hours and forty-one minutes on the street. 750 catalytic texts given. Fifty-eight people stopped and spoke with me. Sixteen gave me their signatures and addresses, each being mailed a $40.00 check one year later. Project cannot be repeated. Archive in the Caroline Bourgeois Collection.

Welcome home.

An outdoor sculpture, somewhere in upstate New York. I walked off of the "grounds" and found an old building site, then abandoned and overgrown with ferns. Somebody had hoped enough to have a well dug and its opening was covered with an upside-down bucket. Like my previous positive/negative mold-forms, I cast a new well cap out of hydro cal which read "welcome home" and replaced the bucket with it. The cap was left in place after the exhibition and, for all I know, may still be there.

1993. Cast hydro cal. Rushmore Festival, Woodbury, NY. Project cannot be repeated. Documentation in the collection of the artist.

For you for me for painting.

My biggest was the feeling of giving away four years of paintings. Only my collectors knew where but anybody passing by could have one. During the distribution, we re-authored each painting, putting our signatures to their backs. When talking with the participants one year later, each had a different story to tell about what had happened.

Archive begun 1993. Wall St. and Broadway and in Sandra Gering Gallery, New York City. 23 paintings offered. 21 given away. 8 went to strangers who happened to be passing by. 13 went to previous collectors. Only one of the collectors has continued to purchase work. The two paintings left unclaimed went into the archive. Project cannot be repeated. Archive in the Collection of the Frances Young Tang Teaching Museum and Art Gallery, Skidmore College.

Ich werde Ihr schmutziges Geschirr waschen, I will wash your dirty dishes.

On the street, talking with people to discuss the dilemma of the artist as visionary, and seeing if people would invite a stanger into their homes. The test was also to myself, a sort of the flip to "Waffles for an opening." Usually women invited me home, to talk about absent hubands and boyfriends, or to help with chores and children and have some adult conversation during the day. Always, though, the hardest was to say goodbye, us exchanging addresses for some future remembrance.

Archive begun 1994. Munich: Marienplatz (unterfussgang), Pariserplatz and Lindwurmstrasse, Kapuzinerstrasse and Arbeitstrasse, Theresienstrasse and Barerstrasse, Leopoldstrasse and Franz-Joseph-Strasse. Five hours and forty-one munites spent on the street. 1150 catalytic texts given. Eleven strangers' homes visited. Twenty-two hours and thirty minutes spent in these homes. Each participant received a sponge, printed with the project's title and signed by myself and the participant. Project can be repeated. Archive in the collection of the artist.

Bed service.

Trying to relocate the artwork to the maintenance of a hotel, being trained by the housekeeping staff, and becoming invisible. Also, avoiding Sophie Calle, and through their intimacies, the process became anonymous, each room seeing if it was possible to actually assist.

Archive begun in 1994. Phoenix Hotel, San Francisco, during the time of an international art fair being held in the Hotel. Of the twenty-one dealers sleeping in their beds eighteen agreed to participate. Each housekeeper received a photograph. Project cannot be repeated. Archive in the collection of the artist.

Beautiful, Newlyn.

I randomly asked people if what they were doing could be considered sculpture. Then, after videoing them, I taught them to use the camera and they taped me doing the same.

Archive begun 1994. Newlyn, England. Out on the street, in five strangers' homes, in four people's work place, and in a public garden. Ten people participated. A signed copy of the video was made for each participant, five of them taking theirs during the opening and leaving their sinatures behind. Project can be repeated. Archive in the collection of the artist.

Congratulations.

I sent flowers each week of an exhibition, accompanied by a card which read "congratulations." When the curator met me a year later at a party, he said that he had expected me to be "some small, effeminate guy" and apologized for not sending me my promised documentation.

Archive begun 1995. DiverseWorks, Houston. Five bouquets sent. Project can be repeated. Archive in the collection of the artist.

Help.

A collector and I washed his dishes and then signed the kitchen. The price of the project equaled the cost for me to replace my stolen video camera.

1995. A collector's home, Portland, OR. One framed piece that includes text, a stitched-on photograph, and a photograph of the signatures on the collector's kitchen wall. Project can be repeated. Douglas Posten Collection.

Forse, Perhaps.

Barnaba was the one who responded. When arriving at his home one day later, his wife asked if I would wash the upper bank of windows in their home, she being too frightened to climb up that high. I agreed, then three days later cast an object in an edition of two: "arte forse amico" and "art perhaps friend." Barnaba put his on a bookshelf. The other was left at the point where I met him in Campo Santa Margherita. It lasted for ten minutes, until two young boys, amazed that it was not attached to the cobblestones, broke it and ran off with the parts. By the next day, a small child had drawn a multi-pointed star with a chip left behind; then, that evening a rain storm washed everything away.

Archive begun 1995. Residential sections of Venice, Italy. 580 catalytic texts given in one hour on the street. Project can be repeated. Archive in the collection of the artist.

We both belong.

The web as a kind of third sculpture, with two domestic points of reference at either end. After corresponding with me through a threaded bulletin board, participants could mail in a picture of themselves doing their dishes at home. I then framed it with a picture of me doing my dishes and gave it to them. The number of pieces made and given was determined by the resources of the sponsor, äda'web.

Archive begun 1995. In my home, in those of the 23 participants, and at Printed Matter Bookstore. 23 framed diptych photographs given. Website in the collection of the Walker Art Center and currently being hosted at http://adaweb.walkerart.org/influx/kinmont/bk1.html. Project can be repeated. Physical archive in the collection of the artist.

Beautiful.

I videotaped Anne making us a cup of tea.

Anne's house in 1995. Video approximately 6 minutes, unedited. Participant received one signed copy of the video and a second copy in the collection of the artist. Project can be repeated.

Exchange.

Anyone coming into agnes b. could trade the shirt off his or her back for any shirt in the store. Most who I approached thought I was a nuisance and looked to the staff for assistance; when it became clear that I was in earnest, they smiled and quickly found a shirt for themselves. Once the shirt was chosen, the participant and I signed a new label printed with the project's title. Then, I removed the store's label and price tag, and sewed our co-signed label on the new shirt. Next I sewed the store's label and price tag onto the old shirt and then hung it onto the store's racks, as a new agnes b. shirt for sale. While this was going on, participants used the video camera to document the exchange. By the end, half of the people coming in were there by word of mouth. The number of shirts given was determined by how long it took me to do the seam-ripping and sewing.

Archive begun 1995. agnes b. pour hommes, New York City, for three days. The store's seamstress and twenty customers participated. Twenty shirts worth $2,934.00 given. Project can be repeated. Archive in the collection of the artist.

It's easier to talk about art while washing dishes, *Sunderland*.

I had gone downstairs to the City Public Library to ask if I could wash the librarians' dirty dishes. Upstairs, in the Arts Centre, during the opening, I washed these dishes while people videotaped me, chatted, and then signed my body.

Archive begun 1995. Sunderland, England. Seven people brought their their dishes. Eighteen people videoed me, each then signing my body. Project can be repeated. In the collection of the artist.

Antinomian Press.

Needed and unhappy with representation, I began to publish project descriptions. Then, as an agency to support project work, I began to publish work by and about others.

Begun 1995. Project on-going.

It's easier to talk about art while washing dishes, *Wadsworth Atheneum*.

As a lecture for the Atheneum, I showed videos of past projects in the restaurant's kitchen while washing the lunch hour's dirty dishes. Those who came were given a pen that was signed and read: "the object of your authorship." They then videoed me, signed my arms, some helping me to finish the dishes. One woman came up to me halfway through and gave me a pair of rubber gloves she had brought: "I was too embarrassed earlier, but I thought that you might need these."

Archive begun 1995. Wadsworth Atheneum, Hartford, CT. Twenty-seven people attended. Twenty-seven pens given. Project can be repeated. Archive in the Wadsworth Atheneum Collection, purchased with Peter Norton Family Foundation funds.

Somebody's SoHo.

Your philanthropy is our sculpture. Being invited to participate in a group show that had to occur within SoHo, I pointed out the efforts of six community health organization that maintained SoHo addresses. For six days some friends and I sat at tables in the Gramercy Hotel Art Fair, the New Museum, Lucky Strike Restaurant, and Our Blessed Lady of Pompeii street fair. The organizer of the street fair understood the project better than anyone else and offered us a table gratis next to the Mayor's Office and the Church's Senior Citizens Club. It worked best in this context.

Archive begun 1995. New York City. Friends in Deed, Housing Works, Children's Hope Foundation, Gilda's Club, God's Love We Deliver, and the SoHo Partnership participated. 3200 flyers and brochures given. Project can be repeated. Archive in the collection of the artist.

The Materialization of life into alternative economies.

A curated project with people from the art world and showing different notions of economy and distribution: Paula Hayes/Wild Friends for collaborative economy, Joseph Grigely for information economy, On Kawara for gift economy, Gordon Matta-Clark for business economy, and Mierle Laderman Ukeles for maintenance economy. My reasons were to offer another reading of Lippard's idea of conceptual art as a dematerialization of the art object and, instead, suggest that perhaps, for some, it was actually not so much about the art object but about life, about a materialization of life.

1996. Printed Matter Bookstore, New York City. Paula gave away seed packets entitled "cats dig grass;" Carol Goodden (Gordon's collaborator) provided recipes from the restaurant Food, which we gave away photocopies of; and Mierle gave away copies of her *Manifesto for Maintenance Art* from 1969. In the collection of the artist. Exhibition can be repeated.

If you smile at me.

While out running errands one afternoon, I asked people if conversation could be sculpture.

1996. Around Wall St., New York City. 28 minutes in the afternoon with 11 people. The transcribed responses were then printed as an introduction to an exhibition. The exhibition presented work by artists who have conversed with people in non-art spaces as part of their work. The works in the exhibition were by Johannes Baader, Joseph Beuys, Daniel Buren, James Collins, The Rosairo Group, Mierle Laderman Ukeles, and Larionov and Ilya Zadanevich. Artists' pieces dated from 1913–1980 and occurred in Germany, Switzerland, England, Argentina, the United States, and Russia. Exhibition and catalogue printed in an edition of 500 copies; a deluxe version of the exhibition was printed on a few T-shirts. Project and exhibition can be repeated. In the collection of the artist.

Prospectus.

I was there, on the street, to see if someone would loan me an object from their everyday routine. Richard was the one who finally invited me to his home, loaning me two plates for the length of the show. He chose those because they were special to him but also didn't match his usual set. And, if they were sold, Stefano had agreed to split the sale three ways.

Archive begun 1996. 86th and Broadway, 96th and Broadway, and in Basilico Fine Arts, New York City. 501 flyers given in 2 hours and 10 minutes spent on the street. The price of the plates was $3000.00. The plates were unsold and were returned to Richard. Project can be repeated. Archive in the collection of the artist.

Promised relations; or, thoughts on a few artists' contracts.

I was writing my own contracts for ownership and exhibition of the archives. In particular, I was trying to develop an economy of perpetuity, one where I could afford the promises set up in the archives, yet still manage our living expenses. So, I began researching other artists' contracts and *Promised Relations* was the result. Each of the artists was either using the contract as an artwork or as a means to clarify an element in the distribution of their work. It was also the first time I ever offered a group show for sale.

1996–97. AC Projectroom, New York City. An exhibition project with Marcel Broodthaers, Paula Hayes/Wild Friends, Ed Kienholz, Yves Klein, Komar & Melamid, Seth Siegelaub and Bob Projansky, and Various Times and People. Catalogue printed in an edition of 500 copies. Exhibition can be repeated. In the collection of the artist.

Agency.

As a companion to the Antinomian Press I was interested in trying to write a business plan to start an agency to represent project artists. A year or two later Anne Pasternak of Creative Time agreed to provide some funding for me to pursue this idea and see if it would be viable. Unfortunately, the only financial structure which I could see as successful was not one in which I would ever want to participate so the project ended without issue. Through it, though, I began to contemplate the independence of project artists, their marginality (both forced and sought), and the necessity for freedom within an art practice. I was also struck with Anne's disappointment in my decision.

1997. Creative Time is a New York-based nonprofit organization that presents public arts projects in various disciplines. Project cannot be repeated. Archive in the collection of the artist.

The Possibilities of trust as a sculpture and the question of value for each participant.

Invite a stranger into your home for breakfast.

1997. Instruction piece. Collection of those involved.

Vietnam War ads; or, your bibliography is our sculpture.

When doing research for the *Materialization of life* show, I came across an advertisement in Art-Rite Magazine by Carl Andre, Lucy Lippard, and others which read: "Congratulations to the people of Viet Nam." It fascinated me and I found others like it dating from 1965–1975 which I then re-ran as an exhibition in magazines and periodicals. A T-shirt was created as the exhibition catalogue with the ads' original and new bibliography printed in missle-red.

Project begun 1997. Exhibited in Swedish magazines and periodicals as an exhibition within an exhibition by Carlos Basualdo entitled "Insertions" and at various museums in Stockholm, 1998. Exhibition can be repeated. In the collection of the artist.

The Third sculpture, or thoughts concerning spaces in between.

The work was mostly interactive and ephemeral and concerned with value and participation. It was also simply an accumulation of works by others which were important to me in my thoughts concerning the third sculpture, an idea which I had devised in 1988 to describe my own work out on the street and in strangers' homes. The catalogue was to be made by visitors to the exhibition through their access to the exhibition's archive and a photocopy machine.

Begun 1997. The exhibition was solicited by Independent Curators Incorporated, New York City, but they were never able to find a venue. Work spanned 1960–1997 and was by Yvette Brackman, Stanley Brouwn, Lygia Clark, Christopher D'Arcangelo, Joseph Grigely, Paula Hayes, Lee Lozano, Joe Scanlon, Lincoln Tobier, Jeffrey Schultz, and Ian Wilson. At the invitation of Christophe Cherix, the exhibition was finally presented in published form in the French magazine "Documents sur l'art," no. 12, 2000. In the collection of the artist.

Sometimes a nicer sculpture is to be able to provide a living for your family.

I have started an antiquarian bookselling business to help support my family. The artwork is not the business itself, but the contribution to our cost of living. Because the business specializes in books about food and wine before 1840, it also provides a broader context in which to see domestic activity as meaningful. So far it has been successful.

Begun 1998. New York City. Books sold concern food, wine, domestic economy, and nutrition. Project on-going. In the collection of the artist.

A Footnote exhibition.

A curated project within a curated project, organized by Dario Robleto
for Artist Space. I was thinking of precedents for interactive work and
listed the following three actions on a piece of paper to present them as a
group show. The sheet was push-pinned onto the wall, but it could have
simply been placed on the floor of the exhibition space.

- James Collins. Introduces two complete strangers to each other in
  Hyde Park. "Introduction Series." London, 26 May, 1970.
- Lee Lozano. Takes a jar containing bills of $5, $10, and $20 and offers
  it to guests in her house, documenting their responses. "Real money
  piece." 3 April–9 July, 1969.
- Lygia Clark. Cuts a Möbius Strip, inserts her hand in one end and
  Hélio Oiticica's in the other, holding the two of them together. Lygia
  Clark and Hélio Oiticica, "Dialogue," 1966.

1998. New York City. Exhibition can be repeated. In the collection of
the artist.

Sometimes.

Noting their authorship as participants and trying to close the chapter on Yves Klein's signing the model's body.

I went across from the Museum to wash dishes in the restaurant Le Petit Diable. After eating, people brought their dishes from the dining room to the kitchen and videotaped me while I washed their dishes. Afterwards each signed my body and the room in which they ate. I also signed the room and to my knowledge, the signatures, with a project description, remain in the restaurant.

Archive begun 2000. For Les Abattoirs, Art Moderne et Contemporain, Toulose, and Le Petit Diable Restaurant. Dishes washed for two days, approximately six hours each day. During the length of the exhibition, a copy of the videotape played in the restaurant. Archive in the collection of the artist.

Just.

During the time of a museum benefit show, the following was written on an exhibition wall: "Write a check to the New Museum for any amount. When the check is received, it will be stamped in the memo section with the project's title and artist's signature, and then deposited. Upon its return to you from the bank, you can frame the check and hang it on the wall as an artwork. Your philanthropy is our sculpture."

2000. New York City. Stefano Basilico wrote the text on the wall of the New Museum for me. Project can be repeated. In the collection of the artist.

Moveable type no documenta.

In my backpack I had reams of paper and a portable printer, scanner, and computer. Ten different people agreed to participate. With each person I spent a day, speaking about what was the most meaningful thing in their life; how that meaning was created; could that meaningful thing be understood as art; *should* it be understood as art; and, then, finally, what was the difference between that meaningful thing in their life and what they experienced in the museum. The sequence of the questions was important and even though they were all Kassel residents, only one had ever been to visit Documenta.

I took notes in German and English, transcribed them into a laptop, and then asked each participant to proofread what I'd written. Once corrected, I printed the text with a battery-operated printer and then distributed the flyers in the participant's neighborhood. One full day was devoted to each conversation and its distribution.

Archive begun 2002. Kassel, Germany. Ten people participated, including one middle school teacher who chose to include her 12-year old students. At each participant's location, approximately 200 flyers were distributed. Later, in the museum during the one hundred days of Docummenta and using the same equipment and type of paper that we used on the street, we printed and distributed 15,000 sets of the flyers, each representing a group show of ten conversations in Kassel. Project can be repeated. Archive in the collection of the artist.

Shhhh.

Still I was wondering about the fragile meanings created at home, and how one can create work about, or in reference to, these delicate moments yet without their destruction.

So, I invited people living in Chatou to have a conversation in their home, amongst themselves, and to consider the possibility of this conversation as a work of art. Before, in the museum, I spoke about past projects and historical precedents for conversation as sculpture. The families who wanted to participate then went home, each later notifying me by email to say when they had had their conversation. The content and nature of each conversation remained a secret known only to them.

Afterwards, I made each family an engraving. The plate's impression on the paper was blind with the exception of the family's name and the date of their conversation. At my request each family chose the size and color of their engraving and four impressions were made of each: one for the participant, one for the museum, one for the Bibliothèque Nationale, and one for myself.

The engraving does not document the content of the conversation. It tells only that there was a conversation had by a family on a certain day. However, it does function as an art object, as something to be exhibited and which can circulate within the art world. For those within the family, the engraving is more: it comes out of a domestic moment and functions as an *aide memoire* for a conversation once had.

2002–2003. 23 families participated. Centre national de l'édition et de l'art imprimé, Chatou, France. Project can be repeated. Prints in the collections of the families, CNEAI, Bibliothèque Nationale, and the artist. Archive in the collection of the artist.

Inclusion full-up.

Everyone is invited and knows. We become a facilitator to ask about the slide registry as a document and where representation is located in such a large invitation. The gallery gives and contains, as it produces a catalogue and the dinner is occasioned by a space filled with the works of those who participate. These elements are all parameters of our current curatorial dilemma, a type of awkward democracy where we try to include all in an environment more familiar with exclusivity, this attempt more of an impossible possibility than a conclusion.

2003. An unrealized project with the Moore College Gallery slide registry and exhibition space. The slide registry contained thousands of local artists' work and contact information, and each artist was to be invited to exhibit a work and come together for a dinner. My proposal was made at the invitation of Carlos Basualdo and Reinaldo Laddaga. Project can be realized elsewhere. In the collection of the artist.

This is not art.

Jacob Fabricus asked if I would design a sandwich board for him to wear around the streets of Brooklyn, so I suggested he print one up that read "This is not art." He then spoke with passersby about the idea of his show, the reason for the sign, and what people thought art could and couldn't be.

2003. Fulton Mall between Adams Street and Flatbush Avenue in Brooklyn on one day. Jacob's project was sponsored by the Wrong Gallery and the Public Art Fund. Project can be repeated. Sandwich boards in the collection of the artist.

The Digger dug.

Looking back at myself, I wondered if it was possible to help others through an art practice and how a move outside of the institution might benefit or complicate that effort. So I spoke with a friend who was a social worker to ask for her thoughts on this question, and to hear what she saw as the difference between a professional social worker and an artist who wants to help someone through their work. She answered that it was actually difficult for an artist to help another because the concept of authorship was an obstacle: nobody participating in a project would want to be "authored" by another, no matter what the purpose. She also noted the difficulty for artists to have a meaningful effect on others due to the brevity of most artists' commitment to a given social cause.

Later, in 2006, I worked with my students on the same question, eight in France and eight in the United States, each of whom conducted their own project addressing this issue. In France, the students noted the various ways in which helping others "can create new possibilities of human exchange" while also creating a "risk factor [which] is much higher than in most forms of object-making because another's life is directly involved." The American students were more concerned with issues of sincerity and whether it was the role of art to "unpack" the complications of trying to help another.

Archive begun 2004. Sebastopol, CA. Descriptions of the student's individual projects and conclusions can be found on the two "Student Series" Antinomian Press publications sutbitled "considerations towards helping others in an art practice." Project can be repeated. Archive in the collection of the artist.

This isn't it.

A visitor passes through a museum, finds a spot, and while blowing up a balloon, thinks of something that isn't art. The balloon is dropped, the visitor signs the nearest wall, and then leaves.

2004. ICA, London; Musée Art Contemporain, Lyon; Muzeum Sztuki, Lodz, Poland; CAC Contemporary Art Centre, Vilnius, Lithuania; Kunstihoone, Tallinn, Estonia; and Bizart, Shanghai, China. Project can be repeated. Letterpress envelope and documentary photographs in the collection of the artist.

Also.

I searched for the not-for-profit organization nearest to the gallery. It was a few blocks away and was an *association* which trains dogs for those living with handicaps. At the director's home, I described my project and how the proceeds of the sale would go to the cost of one dog. I also explained that the gallery had agreed to give 100% of the proceeds to the *association*.

Upon four small canvases was watercolored "there is also a need outside of here." Although this work was similar to others in the show, this was the only piece that would result in a donation. The collector's action would have an effect on a local organization that was set up to help another in need, thus changing the meaning of the purchase.

Afterwards, I had a very interesting debate with friends about the difference between what philanthropy means in France and the United States, and the role of the State to provide for those in need.

2005. Association Nationale pour l'Education de Chiens d'Assistance pour Handicapée and Air de Paris. The work went unsold. Project can be repeated. In the collection of the artist.

On becoming something else.

The difficulty lies in oneself, and its relation with the outside. A person can follow an idea, question and develop its course, and even though it will start in one place, it can easily end up somewhere else. But then how do we know it is elsewhere? Is the practice simply an extension of what had happened before, or has it become something else? In some art practices this process of identifying it as something else is necessary in order for the activity to be understood in the new place one finds oneself, perhaps by the people the activity is seeking to address, or assist. But always there is the question of what it has become and the points of reference we use to define it as such.

For this project, I wrote seven paragraphs to describe the work of seven different artists. Each of these artists had pursued an art practice that eventually led them out of the art world and into something else. In some cases it was permanent, in other cases temporary. But it was important to me that the new thing they were doing was an extension of their previous practice, not simply a decision to give up.

Cooking is the act of ingredients becoming something else, something to be eaten and shared. For the current project, I asked various chefs in Paris to write recipes to represent the paragraphs as well as be homage to the artist who made the decision to leave the art world. When speaking with the chefs we discussed the possibilities and impossibilities of recipes and representation as well as the history of its most flamboyant example, the *pièce montée*: sweet and savory edible sculptures created by chefs to represent past events and forms of architecture. Although the *pièce montée* began in the 17th century and continues today, it reached its apogee in the 19th century with the recipes of Antonin Carême and Urbain Dubois.

From the beginning, I had conceived of this project in two forms. In the first iteration, I would organize a private dinner for friends and with one chef only. For the second version, I would work with a museum, involve many different chefs and restaurants, and thereby be able to make the project available to a large number of people.

On becoming something else *in private*.

For the private dinner I worked with Fabien Vallos as chef. For this evening, I asked Fabien to write one recipe for each of the seven paragraphs and to keep in mind that the seven dishes together would constitute a meal to be served to about thirty of our friends. The dinner was held at Le Chapeau Melon, a restaurant I visited regularly in the Belleville neighborhood of Paris. Olivier Camus, the owner, kindly let us use the place for one night and Linda Grabe and Florence Bonnefous helped with the wine and service while I washed the dishes and Bruno Serralongue photographed the event.

During the dinner I also distributed a letterpress broadside printed as a keepsake as well as an essay by Félix Fénéon entitled *La Plastique Culinaire*. Published by the Antinomian Press with an introduction by Fabbien Vallos and a translation into English by Rachel Stella, Fénéon's essay was first published in 1922 and is an early history of the *pièce montée* and their chefs, whom Fénéon referred to as "les sculpteurs et architectes à toque blanche." This was the first edition of Fénéon's essay to be be published in English.

Archive begun 2009. Paris. The broadside was printed in an edition of 200 copies and included the seven paragraphs, Fabien's recipes, and some general text about the project. Project can be repeated. In the collection of the artist.

On becoming something else *in public*.

For this collaboration I worked with Linda Grabe and Florence Bonne-fous to help find and approach seven different chefs to participate. I asked each chef to select one of the seven paragraphs and construct a recipe for its representation. In this process they had complete freedom. I also asked that they insert the dish into their restaurant's regular menu and make it available to anyone coming into the restaurant during time of the project's exhibition. In this way, visitors to the museum would have to leave the institution to experience the paragraph's representation while at the same time regular visitors to the restaurant could participate without even knowing it.

In the museum I distributed a new version of the menu broadside, updated to include the names of the chefs and their restaurants as well as a list of the recipes and the corresponding biographical paragraphs. Both the broadside and the Fénéon essay were given away for free in the exhibition space. Additionally, I had made a bibliography of the works Fénéon (sometimes obliquely) cited in *La Plastique culinaire* and borrowed them from the Bibliothèque Nationale. These, along with some descriptive text I had written about the books, were shown in a large vitrine alongside the broadsides and Fénéon's publication.

Archive begun 2009. Paris. Exhibition took place at the Pompidou and was organized with the support of Air de Paris. 5,000 copies of the broadside and 2,000 copies of *La Plastique culinaire* were printed and distributed for free during the exhibition. The participating chefs and restaurants were: Inaki Aizpitarte at Le Chateaubriand, Yves Camdeborde at Le Comptoir du Relais, Olivier Camus at Chapeau Melon, Raquel Caréna at Le Baratin, Alain Passard at L'Arpège, Jérémy Rosenbois at Cru, and Robert Vifian at Tan-Dinh. Project can be repeated. Archive in the collection of the artist.

PLATES OF ARCHIVE DOCUMENTS

9.95.95.51
15.95.96.43.1
1.90.91.22.2
4.92.94.34.1
4.92.92.2
2.91.92.5
13.95.95.17
16.96.96.7.2
8.94.95.17
9.95.95.13
1.90.91.7
10.96.96.22
13.95.95.11
6.94.94.16
13.95.95.20
11.95.96.9

Per favore
tratta I materiali d'archivio
con cura

Please
handle the archive materials
carefully

Children's Hope Foundation
  help to children
  with HIV and AIDS
  Contact Liza Josephson
  at 979-9206

Friends in Deed
  emotional, spiritual,
  and psychological support
  to those affected by a
  life-threatening illness
  Contact John Juska
  at 925-2009

Gilda's Club
  a free cancer support
  community
  Contact Diane Carnet
  at 647-9700

God's Love We Deliver
  nutritional support
  services for people living
  with HIV/AIDS
  Contact Melanie Fallon
  at 294-8100

Housing Works
  housing for homeless people
  living with AIDS/HIV
  Contact Susie Park
  at 966-0466, ext. 252

SoHo Partnership
  pre-employment opportun-
  ities for recovering homeless individuals through
  community improvement projects
  Contact Jill Kohler
  at 274-0550

        somebody's soho
        your philanthropy is our sculpture

    YOUR PHILANTHROPY IS OUR SCULPTURE

        bk96

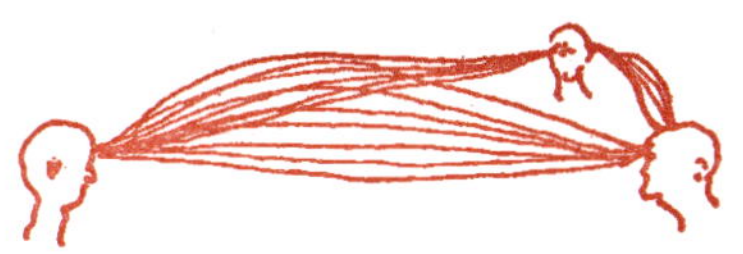

WE ARE THE SOCIAL SCULPTURE!

THIS IS THE THIRD SCULPTURE!

YOU ARE THE THINKING SCULPTURE! *with a variety of cultures, fears and desires,*

From one to another I am for you. We have walked across
~~a field of separation to find you here at this moment and~~
now we would like to share an idea about sculpture, an idea
~~that is both about and for you.~~
In between two ideas there exists a space, a space that is
~~both positive and negative. In terms of drawing and two~~
dimensional thinking, the space is usually understood as an
~~either – or relationship; for example, in the landscape,~~ *where the space*
is either a ~~the space between the factory and the tree is either a~~
gap or the ~~tangible shape or image, or it is "just air", the blank~~
thing itself. ~~space between two important objects of consideration.~~
But when you begin to understand the space in between as
multi-dimensional and that the relationship between or
amongst ideas is dependent upon the ideas themselves, then *we*
~~one~~ can start to discuss and act upon our relationship to
others; that is, we can begin to see that the middle space,
the Third Sculpture, is, in fact, maleable to both an
individual and communal will.

1.90.91.22.2

```
*** U.S. POSTAL SERVICE ***
      CHURCH ST. STA.
     90 CHURCH STREET
----------------------------------
CLERK #02
DATE:   01/12/94  04:24:01 PM
----------------------------------
MO #4975392366
100 MO - DOM              40.00
101 MO FEE-DM               .75
MO #4975392367
100 MO - DOM              40.00
101 MO FEE-DM               .75
MO #4975392368
100 MO - DOM              40.00
101 MO FEE-DM               .75
MO #4975392369
100 MO - DOM              40.00
101 MO FEE-DM               .75
MO #4975392370
100 MO - DOM              40.00
101 MO FEE-DM               .75
MO #4975392371
100 MO - DOM              40.00
101 MO FEE-DM               .75
MO #4975392372
100 MO - DOM              40.00
101 MO FEE-DM               .75
MO #4975392373
100 MO - DOM              40.00
101 MO FEE-DM               .75
MO #4975392374
100 MO - DOM              40.00
101 MO FEE-DM               .75
MO #4975392375
100 MO - DOM              40.00
101 MO FEE-DM               .75
MO #4975392376
100 MO - DOM              40.00
101 MO FEE-DM               .75
MO #4975392377
100 MO - DOM              40.00
101 MO FEE-DM               .75
MO #4975392378
100 MO - DOM              40.00
101 MO FEE-DM               .75
MO #4975392379
100 MO - DOM              40.00
101 MO FEE-DM               .75
MO #4975392380
100 MO - DOM              40.00
101 MO FEE-DM               .75
MO #4975392381
100 MO - DOM              40.00
101 MO FEE-DM               .75
 090 POSTAGE               1.29
 090 POSTAGE                .25
 090 POSTAGE              10.44
 090 POSTAGE               2.50
 109 PVI                   1.34
                      ----------
        TOTAL:    $     667.82
----------------------------------
        *** THANK YOU ***
```

56 Working together has got to be genuine
67 There is no space because we are all one
76 Is it free
79 Do you sculpt

The points of contact between myself + others
My attempt to share and to convince others to share
The vulnerability of being on the street
My opportunity to learn
The openness and unknown

To create my own context
To outline the sculpture's parameters   be critical of
To provide enough information for the viewer to ~~judge~~
me ~~myself~~, the piece, and the public space in which ~~the~~ event occurred

To reveal an existing public sculpture and the possibilities
it contains.

____

During the time of Casual Ceremony visitors to White Columns are invited to join me for a waffle breakfast at my home. If you are interested call me at 212-645-9750. Please bring this paper plate with you. Waffles for an Opening • 13 December 1991-13 January 1992

WE BOTH BELONG

boxes + wrapping
material

framed photographs

couch + coffee table

computer

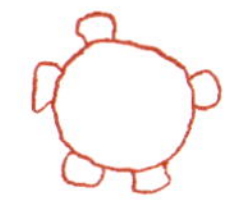

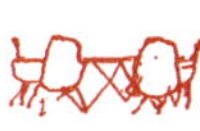

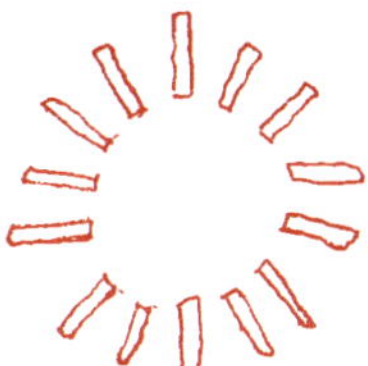

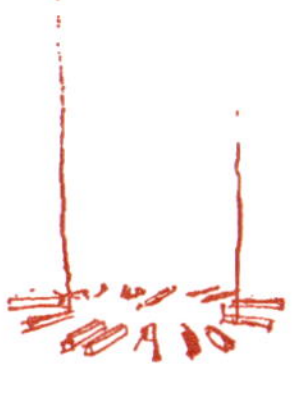

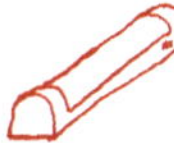

Let us be known by what we believe in. From your home to a
gallery and back again, I am for you. Today, I must find one
person to share some of their dishes as a domestic sculpture
outside of the art world, the share of which is the maintenance
of your life into the economy of a   gallery.

What I am specifically looking for is someone to share afew of
their dishes, dishes which have been washedand will be exhibited
in Basilico Fine Arts for a period of a month. If the dishes are
sold, then the money will be split equally between myself, the
participant, and thegallery deaer. If the piece is unsold at the
end of the exhibition, then the dishes will be returned to the
participant.

If you are interested, please speak with me how. The press
release an the reverse side of this flyer explains the exhibition's
context. Ben Kinmont.nyc.1996.

this original was ~~stolen~~ stolen
from the "Joint Ventures" show curated by
Nicolas Bourriaud at Stefano Basilico F.A.
NYC sometime in Sept./Oct. 1996. The
Gallery didn't notice it was gone. We
didn't either, until inventorying was done
today, 5 Nov. 1996.

Prospectus: archive 16.96.96.7.2*

DISPLAY OTHER SIDE
TO INSURE PRIVACY

Bed service:
archive' 8.34.95.17

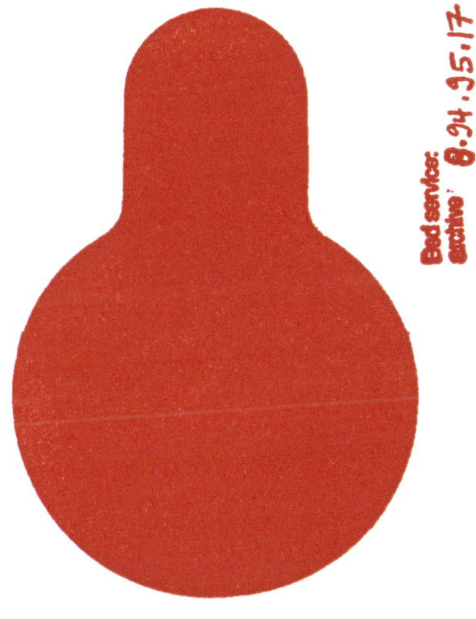

MAID
PLEASE HAVE
THIS ROOM
MADE UP SOON
AS POSSIBLE

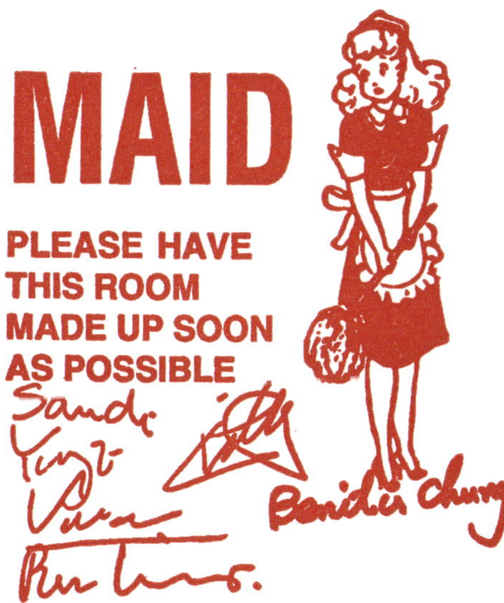

American Hotel Register Company
2775 Shermer Rd., Northbrook, IL 60062
R74-231
1-800-323-5686

→ a pc. done;
practice & preach;
people, & helping
her daughter
Beuys & children

Perhaps

Slow down ~~[crossed out]~~. ~~[crossed out]~~ In so
far as we care for one another, you are my vision
and I am ~~[crossed out]~~ for you. We have come to this place
on our way to something else, on our way to
~~buy~~ buy groceries to see more art, ~~[crossed out]~~ to visit a
friend ~~[crossed out]~~ have a cup of coffee. For these pathways sometimes
cross, as ours have today, and create the opportunity
for bridging a gap that separates the self from
the other. ~~[crossed out]~~

From one idea or moment to another.

I am asking you to help me bridge the gap
which separates the art world from the non-
art world; ~~[crossed out]~~ in so doing, perhaps we can create a situation of trust and
generosity between myself and you.

Perhaps I can help you with a household chore
to ~~[crossed out]~~ ~~[crossed out]~~ ~~[crossed out]~~ share in your daily
responsibilities. Perhaps, in exchange, we could discuss my concern
about the art & life dynamic and you could help me to
make a sculpture.

images: — text of flyer
— street activ.ts
— in home activi:
(incl'd on
the pc.)
— pc on street

8" x 8" x 8" =

with text from interaction + space

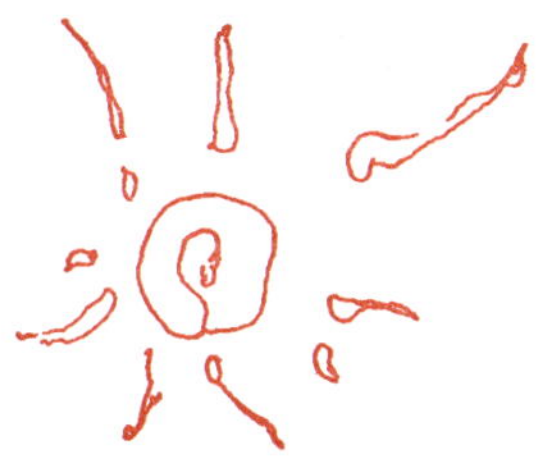

WE ARE THE SOCIAL SCULPTURE!

THIS IS THE THIRD SCULPTURE!

YOU ARE THE THINKING SCULPTURE!

I wish to share an understanding of life. B ut first I want
you to slow down and listen. Notice the fear, the love and
energy that is our sculpture, our community. our communal
creation. We are of that sculpture, we together, you and I, and
those around us.; We are all joint creators, co-creators in
a piece that includes the poor, the rich, the military and
the religious, we must realize that the act of the individual is the act of the community. We mu

You must have some compassion for your self, the other, and
our space that lies in between. because we are a culture
based on the individual, one of private goals and loneliness,
we need to start with the personal, the moments where we
feel fear and joy and create understanding. We must leave
behind Walt Whitman's declaration that "I am a multitude" and
realize that WE ARE A MULTITUDE
               WE ARE A MULTITUDE.

by Ben Kihmont, 1991.

we must learn to accept ourselves as both sculptors and the sculpted. We
must begin to test the point of our lives and ask whither

106

Niomi

called

The piece will be two
photographs of domestic
moments, one of you
washing your dishes and
one of me washing mine,
framed as a diptych
~~photograph~~ and given to
you in appreciation for
your willingness to get
involved.

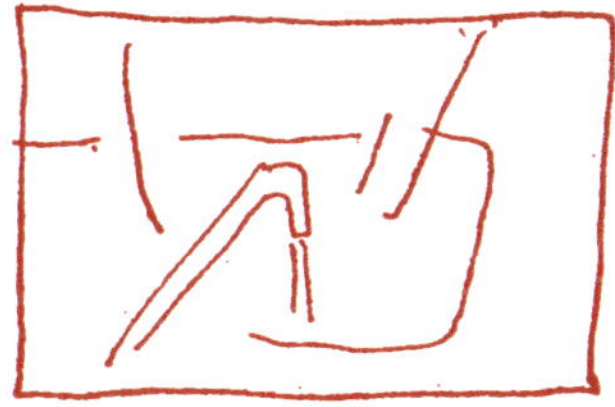

In exchange, I will have
the opportunity to create
a momentary forum where ~~I~~ we
can explore new ways of
creating artwork and
~~_____~~ an alternative
means of economy, where
the location of value ~~and~~
~~the will to participate~~
depends upon these
participants involved.

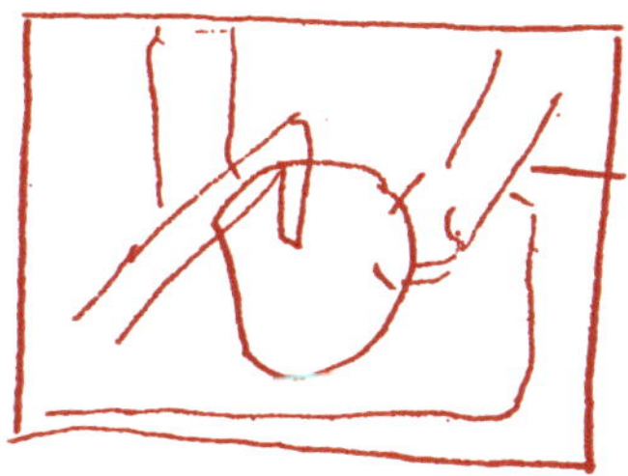

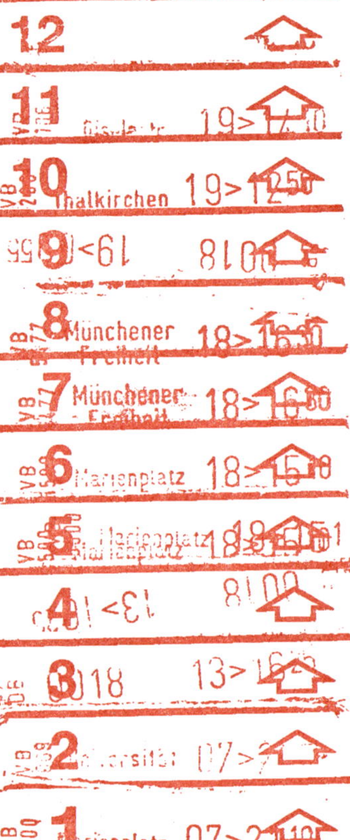

12
11 Giselastr. 19> 17.40
10 Thalkirchen 19> 12.50
9 <19 8018
8 Münchener Freiheit 18> 16.30
7 Münchener Freiheit 18> 16.30
6 Marienplatz 18> 15.00
5 Marienplatz 18> 15.51
4 <13 8018
3 8018 13> 16.00
2 Universität 07>
1 Marienplatz 07>21 40

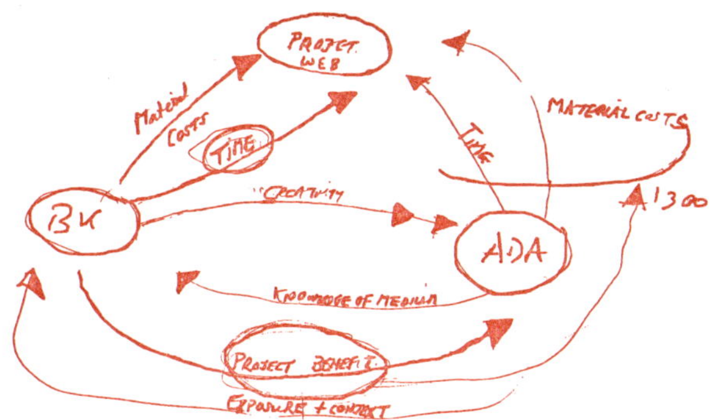

PROJECT WEB
Material Costs
TIME
CREATIVITY
MATERIAL COSTS
BK
ADA
Time
1300
KNOWLEDGE OF MEDIUM
PROJECT BENEFIT
EXPOSURE + CONTEXT

what is exchanged?

F. CLAUDE KNEE
608 474 (X)
609 921 8218

Fishing for participation. Willingness
to get involved.

who is this guy?

No thank you. But
thanks anyway.

7 Word of mouth ⟶
3 overhearing ⟶
3 curiosity ⟶
This is my favorite shirt (2)

Exchange: archive 11.95.96.9

APPENDIX

Our Contract;
or, some thoughts on archive ownership and exhibition.

I have written the following sentences in an effort to clarify how I view
the archive as a work of art to be collected, maintained, exhibited, and
used by others.

Like the projects themselves, the archives have no single moment or
object that is the archive.

The archive is, instead, an accumulation of materials and traces.

It is a map of the project with a beginning and an open end.

It is a collection of documentation that is a context for watercolors,
drawings, and sculpture as well as contracts, bills, notes,
correspondence, and receipts.

It is an invitation for future interaction.

It is a system that emphasizes custodianship of a given idea or work
and as such, it supports the collector's desire to be involved in something he or she finds interesting.

It is a means for a collector or institution to encourage another's
practice through an act of patronage.

It is a way to make transparent the project's formulation and to show
who was involved.

It is a form through which to observe a project in both its profound
and boring aspects.

It is a place in which to bring things together without heirarchy.

It is an opportunity to understand what has happened.

With these thoughts in mind, I would like to point out the following: after ownership, material can be added to the archive to continue mapping the project's use and meaning. If such addition occurs, the new objects will be described and included in the archive's inventory list and numbered accordingly (see the footnote below). If the owner sells the archive to another individual or institution, the owner must notify the artist's representative and when such a change of ownership occurs, this text will accompany the archive and be brought to the new collector's attention. It should also be noted that the archive can never be broken up to sell to individual items.

Each item in the archives is assigned a number that follows a specific system. For example in the *Exchange* archive, there is a document numbered 11.95.08.55. This number means that that particular document is from the 11th project to have an archive; the project was begun in 1995; this particular item was added in 2008; and it is the 55th object in the archive. The purpose of this cataloging system is to give an individual item a relation to the larger whole as well as make it possible for a collector or registrar to identify a particular item.

Distributed by
JRP | Ringier
Letzigraben 134
CH-8047 Zurich
T +41 (0) 43 311 27 50
F +41 (0) 43 311 27 51
E info@jrp-ringier.com
www.jrp-ringier.com

ISBN 978-3-03764-169-9

JRP | Ringier publications are available internationally at selected
bookstores and from the following distribution partners:

Switzerland
Buch 2000, AVA Verlagsauslieferung AG, Centralweg 16, CH-8910
Affoltern a.A., buch2000@ava.ch, www.ava.ch

Germany and Austria
Vice Versa Vertrieb, Immanuelkirchstrasse 12, D–10405 Berlin,
info@vice-versa-vertrieb.de, www.vice-versa-vertrieb.de

France
Les presses du réel, 35 rue Colson, F-21000 Dijon,
info@lespressesdureel.com, www.lespressesdureel.com

UK and other European countries
Cornerhouse Publications, 70 Oxford Street, UK-Manchester M1 5NH
publications@cornerhouse.org, www.cornerhouse.org/books

USA, Canada, Asia, and Australia
D.A.P./Distributed Art Publishers, 155 Sixth Avenue, 2nd floor,
USA-New York, NY 10013, dap@dapinc.com, www.artbook.com

For a list of our partner bookshops or for any general questions, please
contact JRP | Ringier directly at info@jrp-ringier.com, or visit our home
page www.jrp-ringier.com for further information about our program

This book was possible due to the support
of Kunstverein Amsterdam and New York,
the Kadist Art Foundation, Air de Paris, and
the Fales Library at New York University.

The book was designed by Ben Kinmont
and Patrick Reagh. Patrick composed the
book in Monotype Ehrhardt 453 and printed
directly from the metal type. The illustrations
were printed using polymer plates.
The paper is Mohawk Superfine.

A special artist's edition of forty-two copies
has also been issued. This edition is preserved
in an archival box and comes with a signed copy
of the book and one of the project descriptions
composed in metal type.

Published by the Antinomian Press
25 January 2011
1200 copies

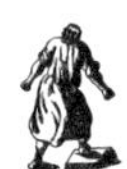